Kings and Queens of Central Africa

Sylviane Anna Diouf

Franklin Watts
A Division of Grolier Publishing
New York • London • Hong Kong • Sydney
Danbury, Connecticut

Note to readers: Definitions for words in **bold** can be found in the Glossary at the back of this book.

Cover illustration by Gary Overacre, interpreted from a photograph by © National Geographic Image Collection

Photographs ©: Art Resource, NY: 31 left (Werner Forman Archive/Anspach Collection, New York), 14 (Werner Forman Archive/Courtesy Entwistle Gallery, London), 21, 26 (Erich Lessing), 12 (Scala); Bridgeman Art Library International Ltd., London/New York: 16 (EX107353/Kongo Kneeling Nkisi Figure. Lower Congo, Central Africa, pre 1889. Carved wood and glass. Royal Albert Memorial Museum, Exeter, Devon, UK), 32 (BCC11160/Bakuba Tribe mask. Wood. British Museum, London, UK); Christie's Images: 48; Corbis Sygma: 39 (Liz Gilbert), 52 (R. Grossman); Corbis-Bettmann: 20 (Ralph Clevenger), 28 (Gianni Dagli Orti), 3 top, 41, 42 (Michael & Patricia Fogden), 50 (Daniel Laine), 3 bottom, 24, 33, 34 (Otto Lang), 29 (Richard Hamilton Smith); Liaison Agency, Inc.: 31 right (Hulton Getty), 8 (Anthony Suau); Mary Evans Picture Library: 10, 12, 15, 19, 22, 27; Musee d'Ethnologie, Geneva, Switzerland: 40, 46; National Geographic Image Collection: 36; National Museum of African Art, Smithsonian Institution: 51, 38 (Eliot Elisofon Photographic Archives, photgraph by Christaud M. Geary); Stock Montage, Inc.: 44; Superstock, Inc.: 43 (Christie's Images), 17, 45; Tony Stone Images: 47 (Paul Harris); Victor Englebert: 6, 11, 49.

Maps by XNR Productions.

Visit Franklin Watts on the Internet at:
http://publishing.grolier.com

Library of Congress Cataloging-in-Publication Data

Diouf, Sylviane Anna
Kings and queens of Central Africa / by Sylviane Anna Diouf
p. cm.— (Watts Library)
Includes bibliographical references and index.
Summary: A survey of the historical regions and kingdoms of Central Africa including biographies of Afonso I, King of the Kongo (1456–1543); Shambo Bolongongo, King of the Bakuba (17th century); and Njoya, King of the Bamum (1867–1933).
ISBN 0-531-20372-7 (lib. bdg.) 0-531-16533-7 (pbk.)
1. Africa, Central—Kings and rulers—Biography—Juvenile literature. 2. Africa, Central—History—Juvenile literature. [1. Kings, queens, rulers, etc. 2. Africa, Central—History.] I. Title. II. Series.
DT352.6.K36 2000
967'.02'0922—dc21 99-086636
[B]

Printed in the United States of America.
1 2 3 4 5 6 7 8 9 10 R 09 08 07 06 05 04 03 02 01 00

Contents

The Kongo Kingdom
The Bakuba Kingdom
The Bamum Kingdom
Modern national boundary
Modern capital city
N
0
500 mi.
0
500 km
Niger
Chad
Sudan
Nigeria
Benue R.
Central African Republic
Cameroon
Bangui
Malabo
Yaoundé
Equatorial Guinea
Congo R.
Ubangi R.
Libreville
Gabon
Congo
Rwanda
Democratic Republic of the Congo
Brazzaville
Kinshasa
Burundi
Atlantic Ocean
Lake Tanganyika
Luanda
Angola
Zambia
Africa
Area enlarged
Atlantic Ocean
Indian Ocean

Chapter One

Kings and Queens of Africa

Africa is a continent of great natural diversity—burning deserts, snowy mountains, lush forests, dry savannas, and majestic rivers. Africa's 800 million people are as diverse as its landscape. Thousands of different populations live in the continent's fifty-three countries. Africans speak 25 percent of the 6,000 languages that exist on Earth.

For tens of thousands of years, Africans have shared the beauty of this vast continent. The peoples used Africa's immense resources while each population developed its own culture, language, and traditions. This amazing diversity could be a source of richness or of division, but from the earliest times Africa has had great leaders who united diverse communities into strong nations.

The kings and queens of Africa were concerned not only with power and the expansion of their kingdoms, but also with justice, education, arts, crafts, agriculture, and trade.

Some ruled in difficult times. The arrival of the Europeans, the rise of the slave trade, and colonization unsettled their territories and entire continent. Rulers faced external threats and internal divisions, and they had to invent ways to govern and protect their communities.

Water from the Lobaye river flows over the Boali Waterfall, in the Central African Republic.

Accounts of the kings and queens of Africa have been passed from one generation to the next through stories and songs. Starting in the eighth century, travelers from North Africa recorded their observations of African rulers in books and letters. Africans, writing in Arabic, did the same, starting in the 1500s. Europeans first arrived in Africa in 1444, and they left records of the rulers and the courts they visited. Natives and foreigners have helped us know the rulers who, with their people, have created the history of Africa.

For the series, *Kings and Queens of Africa*, the continent has been divided into four parts: West, Central, Southern, and East. Each area has characteristics that helped to shape the cultures that developed there. West Africa was a crossroads for trade, and kingdoms and empires based largely on commerce rose in the region. East Africa was molded by the great variety of its peoples. Central Africa was transformed by the migration of the Bantu population from the northwest. Large movements of population changed the course of Southern Africa's history.

Each book in this series looks at different eras to show how the region evolved through time and the most significant rulers of the region. Some were more famous than others, and some well-known figures do not appear here. I have presented social, political, and cultural innovators who connected their kingdoms to a much larger world, defended their territory against foreign invasions, or brought various groups together into one people. These rulers left important legacies.

Today, people still fish in the waters of Central Africa. This man is fishing in the Bay of Luanda.

Chapter Two

The Kingdoms of Central Africa

Twenty-four centuries ago, people speaking Bantu languages came from the Nigeria and Cameroon area to settle in Central Africa. Through the centuries, they farmed the land, growing yams, oil palms, grains, and vegetables. They fished in and traded along the many rivers of this fertile region. In time, they formed villages, chiefdoms, and small kingdoms. Using the local resources such as wood, copper, and iron, they developed refined arts and crafts.

Unlike the people of West and East Africa, the Bantu population of Central Africa did not come into contact with the Arab and Berber traders from the North and was not touched by Islam. The first foreign people to reach the area were Christian Europeans.

The New Kongo of Afonso

Kongo was the most organized and centralized kingdom of the region. Founded in the late 1300s, it thrived for about a hundred years in a purely African environment. But in 1483 the arrival of the Portuguese signaled the beginning of a new era for the kingdom, its people, and its rulers.

The first king who introduced European religion, goods, and technical know-how to the region was Afonso I (c. 1456–1543). But he could not stop the slave trade that eventually sent millions of people from the region to the Americas. Afonso I wanted to deal with Europe on an equal footing, but it was here that the Portuguese established the pattern of deception and exploitation that would mark the story of African-European relations from the fifteenth through the nineteenth and into the twentieth centuries.

In 1770, an observer drew this picture of the people of the Kongo region in Central Africa. Today, people refer to this region as the Congo.

Bakuba: An Innovative State

The kingdom of the **Bakuba** was in the interior. It never reached the fame, wealth, nor power of Afonso's kingdom. But because of its innovative and peaceful ruler, Shamba Bolongongo (seventeenth century), the Bakuba prospered. Shamba's realm gives us an idea of what an African society could be if it developed freely. Without negative forces from the outside, the Bakuba were able to select which foreign elements they wanted.

The Bamum's New Ways

In the mountainous region of central Cameroon live about 570,000 **Bamum**. These people are heirs to a kingdom founded 700 years ago. The most famous of the Bamum kings was Njoya (1867–1933). A restless innovator, he was eager to appropriate, transform, and adapt whatever he found useful in the cultures of his African neighbors and of the Europeans. But Cameroon, more than any other country, was caught between rival European powers and came under the rule of the Germans, the British, and the French. Njoya's fate is symbolic of what the last African rulers faced as they struggled to maintain independence for their people in the twentieth century.

The Kapsikis Mountains in Cameroon

This illustration shows the court of the king of the Kongo in 1491.

Chapter Three

Afonso I, King of the Kongo

Around the year 1456, Mbemba Nzinga, the first son of King Nzinga Kuwu, was born in the kingdom of the Kongo people. This was a vast territory that extended over parts of what are now the Republics of the Congo and Angola.

In 1482, when Mbemba was about twenty-six, an important event took place at the court. The Portuguese, the

Why Portugal?

The Portuguese were the first to explore the Atlantic Coast of Africa. Portugal had no political power in Europe, and the Portuguese were looking for a way to play a role in the continent. One way, they saw, was to become a strong commercial nation. The first Portuguese to sail to Africa were looking for grain and gold. They wanted to replace the Moors and Arabs as intermediaries in the trade between Europe, Asia, and Africa. By setting up trade relations directly with African rulers, they hoped to make huge profits when they sold African goods to the other European nations, and European items to the Africans.

Several centuries ago, an African artist made this bronze plaque showing Portuguese traders or officials who had arrived in Central Africa.

first Europeans in the region, established contact with the king, or the **manikongo**, as his people called him. The Portuguese first sailed to West Africa in 1444, and in the following years they reached the countries farther south. They told the manikongo that they came in peace and wanted only to trade and to bring Catholicism to his people. King Nzinga Kuwu became convinced of their good intentions.

A few years later, he converted. Taking the name Joao I, he became the first Catholic king south of the equator. His son, Mbemba, followed his example and was baptized Afonso in 1491. A year later, Christopher Columbus sailed to America, and this event would have great importance for the Kongo people and their future king, Afonso.

A Time of Trouble

A drawing from 1491 shows the king of the Kongo, perhaps King Nzinga Kuwu, receiving Portuguese missionaries.

By this time things were not going well for the Portuguese in Central Africa. Joao I decided that his conversion to Catholicism was a mistake, so he went back to the faith of his people and his original name, Nzinga Kuwu. His son Afonso, however, was a converted Christian and did not want to abandon his new religion. His father, angry, refused to let him stay at the court. In 1495, the king appointed his son to be governor of the northern province of Nsundi. King Nzinga Kuwu then expelled the Catholic missionaries, but Afonso welcomed them in his province.

Religious Symbols

The Bakongo followed a religion with a supreme god and lesser deities and spirits. To force the people to adopt Catholicism, Afonso ordered traditional religious symbols destroyed.

This ritual object, a kneeling *Nkisi* sculpture, from the lower Congo region, was made in the eighteenth century of carved wood and glass. Nkisi figures are often called power figures.

Afonso remained almost ten years in Nsundi, surrounded by a few of his people who had converted and by the Portuguese missionaries. In 1506, his father died, and the fifty-year-old prince decided to go back to the capital, Mbanza Kongo. The tradition among the Kongo people was that a royal council of eight men and four women elected a new monarch from among the dead ruler's children. To Afonso's disappointment, his younger brother was elected and assumed power. Like his father, he was not a Christian.

Afonso was determined to become king. He gathered a group of thirty-seven Christians to help him. In July 1506, on the eve of the feast of Saint James the Apostle, they entered the capital, Mbanza Kongo. The next day, they attacked the forces of the king. Legend says that a member of the royal council saw a large cross in the sky, the cross of Saint James. He described his vision to the troops, and they became afraid. Afonso's band was victorious, and he claimed that God had displayed the cross of Saint James to help him. He executed his brother, proclaimed himself King Afonso I, and renamed his capital *São Salvador* (the Savior).

Christian Africa

Populations in parts of North Africa, Ethiopia, and the Sudan became Christian between the fourth and seventh centuries. In the rest of the continent, Christianity was introduced by the Europeans in the fifteenth century.

Exploration and missionary work went hand in hand. Christian missionaries accompanied European explorers who wanted to find new resources and trade goods. Many Africans wanted to trade with the Europeans. As people traded, they talked and exchanged ideas, including thoughts on religion. Gradually, some Africans converted to Christianity.

Today, people in Central Africa still practice Christianity. This photograph shows a religious service in Cameroon.

The New Manikongo

One of Afonso's first acts as the new manikongo was to appoint his cousin Dom Pedro de Souza the ambassador to Rome. He sent twelve young men, including his son Henrique, with Dom Pedro de Souza to Italy to study in a number of monasteries. In 1518, Henrique became a bishop and officiated in Rome. He returned home two years later.

Afonso I was eager to spread Christianity through his kingdom. He made Catholicism the religion of the state under the leadership of his son, Bishop Henrique. Afonso built a church in São Salvador. The king also wanted to open schools, build roads, and develop the land. So he asked the new king of Portugal, Manuel I, to send him missionaries, masons, carpenters, physicians, and architects. King Manuel I responded by dispatching only a few missionaries and technicians, some of whom were former convicts.

In just a few months, these missionaries and technicians were all engaged in the slave trade instead of preaching or building houses. They seized or bought Kongo people—some who were supposed to be their allies—and shipped them to South America and the Caribbean islands. There the Kongo people were enslaved on the sugar plantations of the Spanish, French, British, and Portuguese settlers.

Afonso I was furious. He had looked upon Manuel I as a brother. In 1510, he asked Manuel I for legal and military aid, and for officers to control the Portuguese. Manuel I sent only a book of law and an ambassador to act as a military adviser.

The Slave Trade

Between the early 1500s and 1860, 12 to 20 million Africans were shipped to the Americas; between 900 and 1900, 7 million were sent to North Africa and the Middle East. The Portuguese were the first Europeans to engage in this shameful trade. Soon, the British, the French, the Dutch, the Spaniards, the Americans, and the Swedes were also sending African men, women, and children to plantations in the Americas. The raids and wars that led to the enslavement of the people also resulted in millions of casualties. For every person seized, at least one had been killed.

Families were separated forever, and the people who remained in Africa never knew what happened to their loved ones who were shipped away.

In addition to the loss of the millions of people who were taken away, Africa also lost the children they might have had. Therefore, for centuries, as the populations of other continents grew, the size of the African population remained the same.

The slave trade brought social, political, and economic hardship to the continent through wars, migrations, and a freezing of economic development.

The ivory tusks of African elephants were valuable trade goods.

This adviser was a corrupt man who demanded payment for his services in the form of ivory, copper, and slaves.

Afonso Fights the Slave Trade

The manikongo was becoming more and more distressed by the actions of the Portuguese. The missionaries refused to go inland where they were most needed. The craftspeople and the architects neglected their work and devoted themselves to buying and kidnapping men, women, and children.

Slavery had long existed among the Kongo, but once slaves were acquired, they were not sold again, and they were not treated cruelly. However, the Portuguese dealt with their slaves harshly. They were brutal, and often separated family members.

"There are many traders in all corners of the country," lamented Afonso. "They bring ruin to the country. Every day, people are enslaved and kidnapped, even nobles, even members of the king's own family." Every year, 4,000 to 5,000 men, women, and children were kidnapped and shipped to the Americas.

As the manikongo, Afonso had to protect his people. He could not end the slave trade, because Portugal could send warships, but he could try to regulate and limit it. In 1526, Afonso I appointed a committee to make sure that no one was kidnapped and sold into slavery, and that only prisoners of war were shipped to the Americas. The Portuguese slave traders responded by moving their trade far into the kingdom's interior, where it was difficult to control.

Pieces of bronze hardware on Portuguese sailing vessels were used to buy slaves. A large piece could buy a man, and small ones could pay for children.

Iron

In Africa, iron was produced from the eighth century B.C. Iron ore was smelt in clay furnaces that reached more than 1,500 degrees Fahrenheit (816 degrees Celsius).

Afonso's attempt to restrict the slave trade was not working. His people began to lose faith in him and some nobles thought they could disobey him. The situation was becoming dangerous for Afonso, who began to fear for his position, and even for his life. In 1529 and again in 1539, he asked the pope in Rome to forbid the Portuguese to deal in slaves. But there was no response.

A Royal Battle

The Portuguese believed that Kongo had huge reserves of minerals. They sent experts to search for silver, gold, iron, and copper. But Afonso turned them back, refusing them permission to work. He feared that if the Portuguese located the mines, they would invade the country.

To break Afonso's resistance, King Joao III of Portugal—who had succeeded Manuel I—refused to lend the Kongo king the vessels and shipbuilders he needed to maintain trade with Europe. The Portuguese ruler also asked other European kings to stop their commerce with Kongo. As Afonso still refused to cooperate, the Portuguese decided to get rid of him. On Easter Sunday 1540, eight Portuguese tried to assassinate

African Slavery

In Africa, slaves were not considered racially inferior, as was the case in the Americas. Slaves born into a household could not be sold, and only prisoners of war could be purchased. In many cultures, the children of a slave woman and her owner were born free. They, as well as former slaves, could rise to important positions. Some, such as Shamba Bolongongo of the Bakuba, became kings.

him in church. The attempt failed, but the Kongo people were outraged and killed many Portuguese residents in retaliation.

The End of a Reign

Afonso died in 1543, after the longest reign in Kongo history. During his thirty-seven years in power, Catholicism became firmly entrenched in the region. Nevertheless, Bishop Henrique, who died in 1536, could not build a native clergy as he had hoped. After him, most priests and all the bishops in Kongo were Europeans.

Afonso I had welcomed the Portuguese because he believed that they would help develop his country, but his hopes were destroyed. The Kongo people suffered a great deal from the slave trade and from the greed of the Portuguese, and however much he tried, Afonso was not able to protect them.

In 1950, men clean their drums as women sew in a Bakuba village.

Chapter Four

Shamba Bolongongo, King of the Bakuba

Young Shamba Bolongongo had nothing. As the son of a slave woman, he was not considered to be much, either. But unknown to all, Shamba was rich. He was smart, curious, and energetic. Very early, he felt that his village was too

Andop, a royal portrait figure from the early seventeenth century, portrays Shamba Bolongongo, king of the Bakuba, seated in front of a small game board.

small, his world too limited. He wanted to see more and learn more. Accompanied by three slaves, Shamba left his home and began to travel through the lands of the various peoples who lived in what today is the Democratic Republic of Congo (formerly called Zaire). He spent his days observing, asking questions, and experimenting. He talked to the elders, the wise, the farmers, the craftspeople, the herders, and the musicians. Once he was satisfied that he could not learn much more, he left for a new place with his companions, to continue his search for knowledge and wisdom.

The Land of the Bakuba

In the 1620s, Shamba Bolongongo entered the land of the Bakuba, a federation of about twenty closely related groups speaking Bantu languages. They were dominated by the most powerful group, the Bushong. The Bakuba had entered the region about a century earlier to escape the attacks of the Jaga people and the influence of the Portuguese who were established on the African coast.

The Bakuba lived on a vast stretch of savanna south of the equator, in the Kasai region. Shamba decided to settle among the Bakuba. Through his years of travel, his ambition had been growing. Now he set his eyes on the throne. He, the son of a slave, determined to become the next **nyim**, as the Bakuba called their king. How he convinced the people to

The Bantu

Bantu is the plural form of *Mu-ntu*, which means "man." The word designates a group of related languages that are spoken from southern Cameroon through southern and eastern Africa. The Bantu people are from different ethnic groups but are linked by language and customs. Historians trace their origin to the Nigeria–Cameroon area. In the first century B.C., some people left the region and migrated south. Within the next thousand years, several waves of Bantu people settled in central and southern Africa, and spread east toward Burundi and Rwanda. The Bantu migrations had a great impact on the region. The native peoples were pushed south. Bantu languages replaced the native languages, and Bantu agriculture and the techniques of iron smelting—a Bantu specialty—spread through the region.

choose him—an outsider of low status—to be their king is a mystery. Perhaps, because he was a foreigner without links to any clan, he was able to unite different factions against their ruler. He had a reputation as a healer and magician, and this may have gained him support.

However, before he could officially become the nyim, he had to receive the blessings of the royal family. According to local tradition, a new ruler had to be spit on by one member of the clan. This was considered a blessing. Shamba was not sure that anyone in the royal family would bless him, as he was not their choice, so he devised a plan. He hid under a pile of rubbish near the palace and waited for a member of the royal clan to pass by. His plan worked, for one member of the royal family passed by and spat on the garbage, thus blessing Shamba.

An early drawing shows workers grating cassava, an important food of the Bakuba.

King of the Bakuba

Now Shamba was king of the Bakuba, and he set out to use everything he had learned during his travels. To help the Bakuba farmers, Shamba brought three plants imported from the Americas: maize, cassava, and tobacco. These had been cultivated for thousands of years by Native Americans who introduced the plants to the Portuguese. They, in turn, took the plants to Europe and Africa in the sixteenth century. Cassava became one of the most important foods of the Bakuba. Its large white roots are boiled or pounded into flour. Maize, which can easily be stored and preserved, was useful during droughts or when locusts attacked the crops.

Shamba also introduced sorghum and millet, two cereal crops that had been cultivated in other parts of Africa since ancient times. He brought iron tools and better farming techniques, enabling Bakuba farmers to double their production and to improve their diet.

Shamba Bolongongo was a peaceful king who cared about stability instead of about expanding his kingdom. Nevertheless, the Bakuba waged wars when attacked, and their territory did increase. How to govern in the best possible manner was King Shamba's constant concern. He divided his land into provinces, and appointed councilors and ministers for each one. In his capital, Mushenge, he had a prime minister and a Great Council, similar to a modern government. There were two women

Sorghum

Cultivated since ancient times in parts of Africa, this cereal was transported to India and China. The grain is used as a food, like corn, and also to brew beer. Baskets and mats are made with sorghum stems. It is the main food of 500 million people in the world today.

among the ministers. The king also created a corps of officers to maintain law and order. Male officers worked among the men, and thirteen female officers were in charge of keeping peace among the women.

King Shamba worked to help all citizens feel important and respected and not merely subjects without power. He gave titles and special responsibilities to almost everyone. He named judges, soldiers, officers, treasurers, guardians of the gates, bodyguards, and ringers of the royal bell. They all took part in the rituals that marked the political life of the Bakuba kingdom. Each time the king issued a decree or took an action, everyone gathered, dressed in magnificently embroidered costumes. Colorful and joyous parades were held to celebrate the harvests and when new or rare merchandise arrived at the market.

The beautiful costumes of the Bakuba were also Shamba's doing. He showed the people how to weave the leaves of the raffia plant, an art he learned when he lived among a people called the Pende. The Bakuba men wove the raffia so tightly, using narrow vertical looms, that the fabric looked and felt like velvet. Then the women embroidered it with elaborate and beautiful geometric patterns. Neighboring peoples liked the raffia cloth so much that the Bakuba used it to buy goods. They also made wood and ivory carvings, other types of cloth, and iron. They sold these products to acquire copper, pottery, and canoes.

Raffia

The raffia is an African palm tree. Its leaves produce a fiber commonly used to make baskets.

Among the Bakuba people, raffia skirts (left) were woven in sections by men using upright looms (right). The pieces were then sewn together and embroidered by women.

Under King Shamba, the Bakuba controlled important trade routes through parts of Central Africa. The king created a police force that patrolled the roads to see that the goods traveled safely and to collect the taxes he put on imports. Traders were valued by the Bakuba, and Shamba made sure that they lived comfortably.

This Bakuba mask of carved and painted wood, decorated with beads and shells, shows that the Bakuba valued art.

Artists of Bakuba

Artists were a privileged group among the Bakuba. Shamba used his treasury to support the artists so that they could devote their time, energy, and creativity to their work. He opened a center for the arts in Mushenge, and various carvers worked there to create magnificent objects for the royal family. The Bakuba were fond of beautiful designs and patterns. Their baskets, ceremonial masks, swords, bells, stools, cups, spoons, pipes, and tools were all decorated with geometrical designs or representations of forest animals: elephants, antelopes, and leopards. The king's objects were the most beautifully worked of all.

The tradition of carving continues among the Bakuba. A photograph from 1950 shows two craftsmen making a ndop-like figure.

At the beginning of his reign, King Shamba asked a master sculptor to make a sculpture of himself, called a **ndop.** Every nyim after him ordered his own ndop. Each statue was 22 inches (59 centimeters) high and represented the king, sitting cross-legged, holding a symbol of his greatest accomplishment or something important he had done. Shamba chose to be represented with a game board called *lyeel*, which resembles checkers. He had introduced the game to the Bakuba to replace the gambling that was practiced before.

Shamba's Legacy

This 1950 photograph of the king of the Bakuba (center left) shows that he dressed more elaborately than the people in his village.

Shamba was married and, as was the custom in some cultures, had several wives. However, he was unable to have children. To show their respect and affection, his people declared that the capital, Mushenge, was his wife, and thus all children born there were his. They were given his name, which has thus been passed on.

When the king died, his aunt's son succeeded him. Shamba and the son had not been friendly. Unlike Shamba, the son was a warrior who led the Bakuba into many wars against their neighbors.

Shamba was the most popular of the Bakuba kings. His reign was peaceful and prosperous. He remains so well regarded that many legends have sprung up about him. They tell of his supernatural powers. Almost everything the Bakuba have or do is said to have been invented or introduced by this creative man.

King Njoya on his throne in 1931

Chapter Five

Njoya, King of the Bamum

King Njoya was sleeping in one of the hundreds of rooms of his palace, overlooking his city of Foumban in the heart of the country called Cameroon in 1896. He was dreaming. A man was telling him, "Take a slate, and draw the hand of a man. Wash what you will have drawn, and drink the water." In his dream, Njoya obeyed the man. He handed him the

The town of Foumban, capital of the former Bamum Kingdom, in Cameroon

washed slate. The man wrote something on it and gave it back to the king. Many people surrounded them. They all held slates on which they wrote or drew something.

King Njoya woke up. He took a slate, drew the hand of a man, washed the slate, drank the water, and called the people of his court. "If you draw many different signs and give them a name," he told them, "I will make a book." His people were unsure, but Njoya encouraged them: "If you think hard, it will succeed. Go now, and think."

Oral and Written Traditions

Traditionally, the African peoples south of the Sahara preserved their literature, tales, poetry, and history by memory. These were then passed down orally from one generation to the next. In Ethiopia, however, the Ge'ez language was written from the fifth century on, and African Muslims have been using the Arabic script since the eleventh century. Today, people, including these schoolchildren in Cameroon, follow both the oral and written traditions.

A New Writing System

King Njoya dreamed of creating a new writing system with its own alphabet. He grew up seeing books in Arabic, brought to his father by the Muslim **Hausa** traders, but he wanted his people to have their own writing system. He was a proud man and thought that the Bamum could do anything, and do it better than anybody else.

The first alphabet he created with the help of his court had 500 signs. After much simplification, his sixth alphabet had eighty signs and ten numerals. It was called **Shumon.**

This detailed drawing is an illustrated history of the Bamum kings, drawn by King Njoya's son, Prince Ibrahim Njoya.

A Mother's Help

Njoya had the dream in 1896 when he was twenty-nine and had been king, or **sultan**, for five years. He was born in 1867, the son of King Nsangu. When he was twelve, his father was

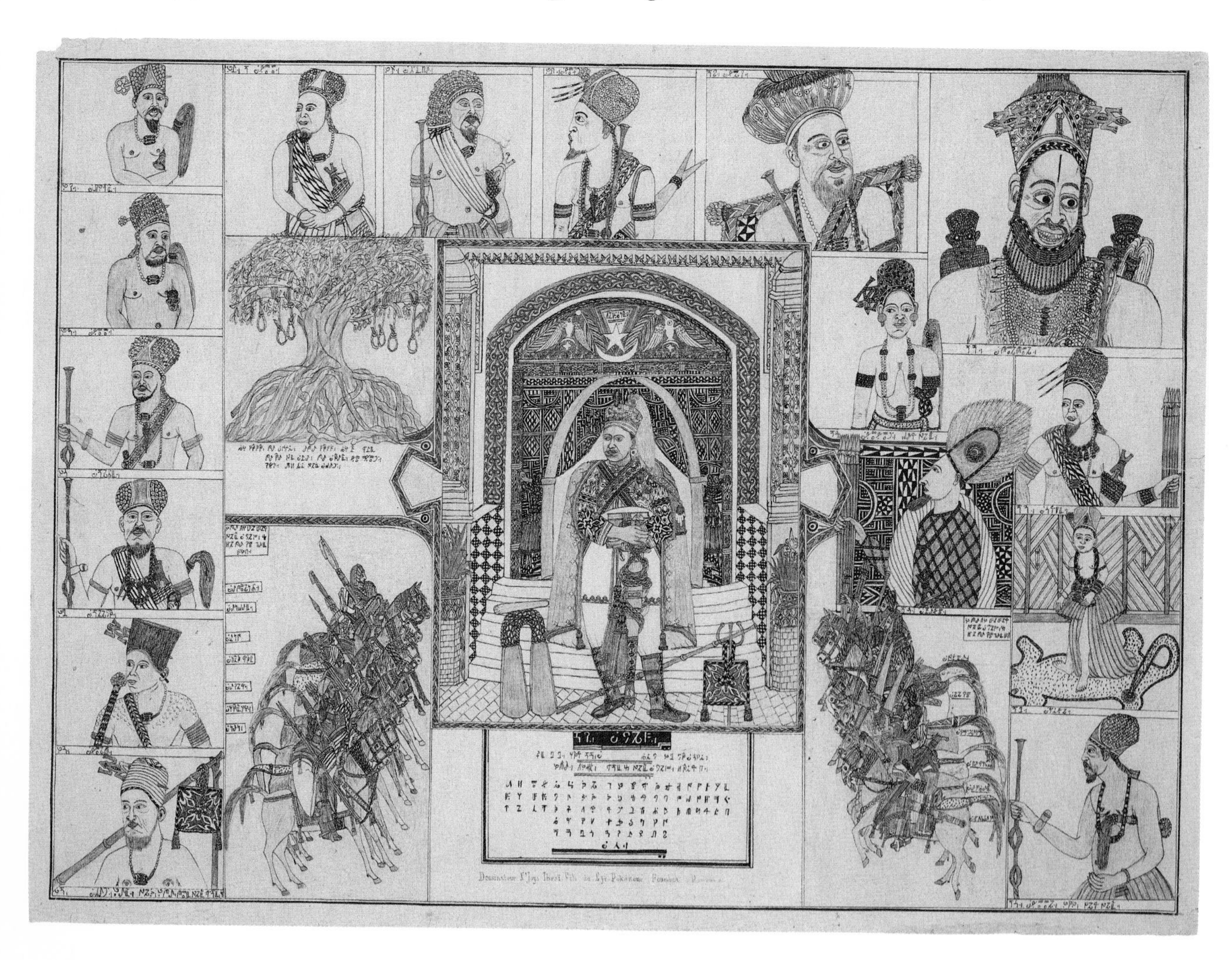

A photograph from the 1990s shows a senior dignitary of the Bamum sultan's court.

killed in battle by his brother, Njoya's uncle, who wanted to seize the throne. The uncle could have succeeded, if not for two women. Njoya's paternal grandmother, Shefton, and his mother, Njapundunke, had vowed that the boy would become the next king. As he was too young to govern, Njapundunke took power and became the **regent**. Njoya was officially enthroned in 1889, but his mother continued to reign until he was old enough to have a child. In Bamum tradition, before a man can become a king, or **mfon**, he has to become a father. Njapundunke was close to her son, and she influenced him a great deal until her death in 1913. When he was absent from his palace, she assumed his role, receiving visitors and making important decisions.

The Fulani

The Fulani people live from Mauritania in West Africa to Cameroon. Their original home was the Senegal Valley, and they spread east in the twelfth century. Traditionally they are herders, but many have settled in towns. The Fulani became Muslims and played an important role in spreading the religion. The Fulani's language, Fulfulde, is spoken by 18 million people.

The colorful uniforms and decorated horses of the Fulani horsemen are still seen in the countryside of Cameroon.

Njoya Is King

In 1894, when Njoya became king, a trusted councilor led an uprising against the royal family. Njoya asked his neighbors, the **Fulani**, to help put down the revolt. With their assistance, Njoya was victorious, and in gratitude he converted to Islam, the religion of the Fulani. He started to wear Muslim garb, a long flowing tunic over wide pants, and a turban.

For years, Njoya and his people lived peacefully in a beautiful region of steep mountains and deep valleys, 150 miles (240 km) from the Atlantic Ocean. Most of the people were farmers who grew groundnuts, sorghum, and corn. The Bamum craftspeople were renowned for their brass casting, ivory and wood-carving, beadwork, and weaving. The capital city of Foumban, with about 20,000 inhabitants, was built 4,000 feet (1,212 m) above sea level. Two ditches, six yards (5.4 m) deep and thirteen miles (21 km) long, surrounded it as a protection against invaders.

A traditional beaded stool of the Bamum, with an animal figure as the base

In 1902, German traders and military personnel arrived in Njoya's kingdom. In 1884, the colonial powers of Europe had met in Berlin, Germany, to divide up the African continent between them, and Germany had claimed Cameroon. Before 1900, the 60,000 Bamum had had no contact with Europeans. Their land was difficult to reach and therefore they had been sheltered from the slave trading of the Europeans.

"One day the whites appeared in the land," Njoya later wrote in his book about Bamum history. "The Bamum said to

Berlin Congress

This meeting was held at the request of the German empire between November 1884 and February 1885. Fourteen countries, including the United States, sent representatives.

They agreed to divide the continent of Africa among France, Great Britain, Portugal, Belgium, Germany, and Spain. Artificial borders were drawn as the European powers saw fit. They divided populations who had always lived together to form separate countries, and forced others who had little in common to become part of the same nation.

Political cartoons, such as the one shown above, pointed out the African struggle against foreign powers. The man on the left carries Uncle Sam.

themselves, 'Let's wage war against them.' 'No!' said Njoya. 'If the Bamum go to war against them, it will be the end of the race. There would be only a few Bamum survivors.'"

After Germany took over his country, Njoya made the most of what the foreigners offered. He started with agriculture. On his two farms, he planted vegetables brought by the foreigners: potatoes, cabbages, tomatoes, barley, and wheat. He was interested in this experiment and looked after the new crops himself.

In 1908, he visited the German governor of Cameroon. King Njoya was impressed by the governor's mansion, but in typical fashion, he did not feel overwhelmed. He was confident that his craftspeople and technicians could do better. A few years later, he set them to work on a large three-story palace in Foumban. Its hundreds of large rooms could accommodate the king's many wives, servants, and **courtiers**.

Crafts had always been an important part of Bamum culture, and the kings

The central market in Yaoundé, Cameroon is one of the places where craftspeople can sell their goods.

had treasures of finely decorated ornaments, jewels, ceremonial pipes, household utensils, and decorative items in ivory, gold, and brass. No other Bamum was allowed to own brass and ivory objects. King Njoya abolished that privilege and allowed his craftspeople to create the same articles for anyone who could afford them. He even opened a store in his palace that displayed the creations of his wives.

Teaching the People Shumon

King Njoya was eager for his people to learn Shumon, and in 1910, he opened a school in his palace for boys and girls as well as for adults. The school was so successful that it attracted more students than the Protestant school run by Swiss missionaries. Njoya's wives were eager students, and a few became teachers. They taught Shumon to other women in the capital. By 1918, King Njoya had opened about twenty schools in Foumban. For the first time, the courtiers recorded births, deaths, marriages, judgments, sentences, taxes, and sales of land.

In this portion of a drawing of Bamum kings (see p. 40), King Njoya holds his book of Bamum.

Njoya set out to create books in Shumon on the history and customs of the Bamum. He and his helpers wrote two books of about 1,200 pages each on Bamum history and traditions. One manuscript was written in a secret language that Njoya developed for his own use. Only he and a few aides knew it. It was like the secret codes used by modern nations.

Another of Njoya's books, written about 1910, was dedicated to medicine and the plants used to cure diseases. He had gathered together all the traditional healers in the area, and questioned them about their knowledge. The first chapter of the book deals with medicinal plants; the second explains childbirth and remedies to ease delivery and help the new mother. How to identify a disease is the subject of the third and fourth chapters. The last two chapters describe how to interpret dreams, and the formulas and prayers to strengthen remedies. This was his most popular book.

Later, the king produced another manuscript to explain a religion he had created, borrowing some elements of Islam. As

Beauty

King Njoya wrote a book on the subject of beauty, giving about 200 standards to measure the beauty of women.

King Njoya used elements from the Qur'an, sometimes spelled Koran, when he created his new religion. The Qur'an is Islam's holy book.

with the writing system, he wanted his people to have something of their own. This failed, however, and the Bamum never followed his new religion. Today, the vast majority of the population is Muslim. Njoya himself returned to Islam in 1917.

Njoya the Innovator

Another of the king's projects was to create a map of Bamum country. A German **cartographer** had explained how to make maps in 1907, and five years later, armed with his memories of this information and his own ideas, Njoya gathered twenty of his people and led them on a **topographic** expedition. They noted every track, crossroad, pond, house, group of trees, and village boundary. The result was a beautiful map of the country, with 1,350 notes in Shumon.

Njoya was also a technical innovator. He and an attendant devised a printing press using Shumon characters, and a mill to grind maize.

Caught Between European Powers

While Njoya was involved in the day-to-day ruling of the kingdom, serious events were taking place in the rest of the world. World War I, in which Germany opposed Britain, France, and their allies, started in 1914. By December 1915, the Germans left Cameroon, and the British and the French took their place. Njoya had assisted the German troops in their few skirmishes against the British in the region, but he was also secretly helping the British enter his kingdom.

Over the years, his relationship with the Germans had soured. The Protestant missionaries had criticized the traditional Bamum way of life and Islam. Njoya felt the Germans were attacking him, his culture, and his people. The king had also become hostile to the German merchants. He accused them of leading immoral lives and objected to their trade practices. They bought ivory and rubber from him at low prices and sold him sugar and fabrics at high prices.

A traditional brass pipe in the Bamum style shows a bearded German soldier.

Cameroon Under French Rule

After the Germans left, Njoya welcomed the British. A short time later, in 1916, France took control of Cameroon. From the start, the French administration and King Njoya clashed. The French insisted that he divorce his wives because polygamy was contrary to their religious and social beliefs. The king let many of his wives go back to their home villages. Then France abolished the tributes that the Bamum people paid to the king. Following custom, he distributed the tributes to the needy and those he wanted to reward. Without this important function, the palace lost its power. In a last blow to the king, France divided his kingdom into seventeen districts and appointed a commander for each one. The new commanders ruled under the leadership of the French, and the king had no more power.

Embittered, Njoya left his palace and spent most of his time on his plantation. He continued his agricultural experiments and finished his Bamum history. But the French wanted to put a complete stop to his influence. They ordered him to stay on the plantation permanently. Njoya refused and in 1931, they exiled him to Yaoundé, the capital of Cameroon. He died there on May 30, 1933.

Polygamy

Polygamy is the practice, still legal in certain countries, to have more than one wife or, much less commonly, husband at the same time. As was customary for Central African kings of his time, Njoya had several hundred wives.

The city of Yaoundé, in Cameroon, where Njoya spent his last years

A son of Njoya, Seidou Njimoluh, became king of the Bamum in 1933.

France hoped to abolish the royalty, but the Bamum insisted that they wanted a new king. The French realized that a friendly ruler with only moral authority could be useful. So on July 3, 1933, one of Njoya's sons, Seidou Njimoluh, was placed on the throne. His reign was the longest in Bamum history, and today, one of Seidou's sons, Ibrahim Mbombo Njoya, is sultan. His role is to be an adviser to his people. He does not reign as a king, since Cameroon is a republic with an elected president.

Ibrahim Mbombo Njoya still lives in the palace built for his grandfather, King Njoya. Part of the palace is a museum that Njoya started in the 1920s, to display his manuscripts and the rich cultural heritage of the Bamum.

Njoya is remembered as one of the most innovative African rulers. His success in using and modernizing traditions and adopting useful foreign ways gained him admiration and respect.

Foumban

King Njoya's palace in Foumban is the most visited historical place in Cameroon. Foumban is also the center of modern Cameroon's tourism and craft industries. The beautiful crafts of the Bamum—brass casting, cloth weaving and dyeing, wood and ivory carving, and beadwork—are known throughout the world.

Kinshasa, the capital of the Democratic Republic of Congo, is the country's largest city.

Chapter Six

Central Africa Today

After centuries of a glorious past and seventy-five years of often brutal French, Belgian, German, Portuguese, and Spanish colonization, Central Africa has had a turbulent and painful recent history. Coups, civil wars, dictatorships, and secession attempts have scarred some of the countries in this region.

The area's extraordinary wealth in diamonds, oil, wood, gold, and other precious minerals has been a blessing, but it has also created problems. As in the past, native and foreign special interests continue to try to gain control of Central Africa's riches—and generally succeed, to the detriment of the majority of its population.

With about 90 million inhabitants, the nine countries of Central Africa have the lowest population density of the continent. However, they also have the highest birth rate, and the number of Central Africans is expected to double within the next twenty-five years.

More than ever, the region will need the strength and wisdom of leaders such as the kings and queens who brought innovations, good administration, and prosperity to the land.

Glossary

Bakuba—a people living in the Democratic Republic of Congo. *Bakuba* is plural; *Kuba* is singular.

Bamum—a people living in the central part of Cameroon. Bamum is also the name given to their ancient kingdom.

Congo—see Kongo

cartographer—a mapmaker

courtier—an attendant at the court of a sovereign

Fulani—a large and widespread African people. *Fulani* is the plural of the name, and the singular is *Pulo*.

Hausa—an African people living in Cameroon, Niger, and Nigeria

Kongo—a people living in Central Africa, as well as their kingdom and the large river, now called Congo, that flows in the region. Today, two countries also bear the name Congo: the Republic of Congo and the Democratic Republic of Congo (formerly Zaire). The inhabitants of both countries are called the Congolese. Some Congolese are of the Kongo ethnic group; others are Bakuba or from other groups. *Ba* is used to make words plural, so one person is a Kongo, two are called Bakongo.

manikongo—king of the Kongo people

mfon—king of the Bamum people

ndop—a small sculpture representing the king of the Bakuba

nyim—king of the Bakuba

regent—a person who rules during the absence of a sovereign or when the sovereign is too young to govern

Shumon—the alphabet of the Bamum people

sultan—an Arabic word meaning the king or ruler of a Muslim people

topographic—having to do with detailed physical features of a region

To Find Out More

Books

Cameroon. Minneapolis, MN: Lerner, 1999.

Central African Republic. Minneapolis, MN: Lerner, 1996.

Finley, Carol. *The Art of African Masks.* Minneapolis, MN: Lerner, 1999.

Heale, Jay. *Democratic Republic of the Congo.* New York: Marshall Cavendish, 1999.

Jordan, Manuel. *The Kongo Kingdom.* Danbury, CT: Franklin Watts, 1999.

Leuchak, Rebecca. *The Bakuba.* New York: Rosen Publishing Group, 1997.

Mann, Kenny. *African Kingdoms of the Past: Kongo, Ndongo.* Parsippany, NY: Dillon Press, 1996.

Ndukwe, Pat I. *Fulani.* New York: Rosen Publishing Group, 1996.

Okeke, Chika. *The Kongo.* New York: Rosen Publishing Group, 1997.

Organizations and Online Sites

Africa: The Art of a Continent: Central Africa
http://artnetweb.com/guggenheim/africa/central.html
Go to this nested page within the Guggenheim Museum site to learn more about the art of Central Africa.

Background Notes: Cameroon
www.state.gov/www/background_notes/cameroon_9912_bgn.html
The U.S. Department of State maintains this site, which includes information about the history, people, government, and geography of Cameroon.

Kings of Africa
http://www.tamarin.com/kings/kindire1.htm
See many photographs of African kings at this site.

The National Museum of African Art
950 Independence Avenue, SW
Washington, D.C. 20560
http://www.si.edu/nmafa/
Part of the Smithsonian Institution, this museum promotes understanding of the diverse cultures in Africa through the visual arts.

San Francisco African American Historical and
Cultural Society
Ft. Mason Center – Building C
762 Fulton Street
San Francisco, CA 94123
The society presents educational programs on the history and culture of African and African-American people.

A Note on Sources

In writing *Kings and Queens of Central Africa*, I consulted several sources. Some were in French, as the two Congos and Cameroon are French-speaking countries. These sources include *The General History of Africa* (eight volumes), published by UNESCO and the University of California Press; *Correspondance de Dom Afonso, roi du Congo 1506–1543* by Louis Jadin; *Great Rulers of the African Past* by Lavinia Dobler and William Brown; *Historical Dictionary of Congo* by Samuel Decal et al; *The Children of Woot* by Jan Vansina; *Le royaume Kuba* by Jan Vansina; *Historical Dictionary of the Republic of Cameroon* by Mark W. DeLancey; *Images From Bamum* and *Things of the Palace* by Christeaud Geary; *L'écriture des Bamum* by Idelette Dugast; and *Kings of Africa* Erna Beumers, ed.

—*Sylviane Anna Diouf*

Index

Numbers in *italics* indicate illustrations.

About the Author

Sylviane Anna Diouf is the author of fiction and nonfiction books for adults and children and of numerous articles for international publications. She specializes in the history of Africa and of people of African origin.

Of Senegalese and French parentage, Ms. Diouf has lived in various African and European countries and in the United States. She has traveled in many parts of the world and speaks several languages. She holds a doctorate from the University of Paris and lives in New York City with her son.